Psyche Matters

A Journey into Mental Health, Well-Being, and Self-Care

By

Winifred C. Brandon

Table of Contents

INTRODUCTION

Hello dear! Life's a wild ride, right? Between school, companions, and the hurricane of feelings, feeling like we're amidst an inestimable storm is simple. Welcome to "Psyche Matters," an aide planned only for us, as we explore the ups and downs of being a teen.

In these pages, we will disentangle the secrets of our psyches. Consider it a tool compartment for understanding the reason why we feel the manner in which we do and, all the more critically, how we can guide our psychological boat through rough waters.

We'll start things off with "The Lowdown on Sentiments." It resembles unraveling the messages our feelings send us. From the energy of pounds to the disappointment of tests, we'll investigate everything. Prepare to become feeling investigators!

In any case, stand by, there's something else! We'll jump into the universe of "Taking care of oneself Systems." Forget the adage; this isn't just about bubble showers and scented candles (albeit those are extraordinary as well). We'll uncover pragmatic ways of being our own legends, guaranteeing our psychological shield areas of strength, to be prepared for whatever might happen.

Thus, individual explorers, lock in for an excursion into the core of teen hood. "Psyche Matters" is your identification to grasping yourself, overcoming difficulties, and arising as the staggering people you are. Allow the investigation to start!

Part 1: The Lowdown on Sentiments: Exploring the Close to home Scene

In this section, we'll set out on an excursion to grasp the complex scenes of our sentiments — the highs, the lows, and in the middle between. Lock in as we explore the lowdown on sentiments, disentangling the intricacy of our profound encounters.

**1. The Profound Range

Sentiments resemble the shades of a clear rainbow, painting the material of our lives with a large number of tones. From the glow of euphoria to the cool wind of happiness, and the blustery billows of trouble to the lightning strikes of energy, every inclination adds profundity and wealth to our human experience.

**2. The Back and forth movement

Feelings are not stale pools, they are waterways that stream and develop. The back and forth movement of sentiments are normal, similar as the evolving tides. It's fundamental to perceive that encountering a scope of feelings is an indication of a rich and dynamic inward life.

**3. The ability to appreciate individuals at their core

Understanding and exploring our feelings is an expertise worth sharpening. The ability to appreciate individuals on a profound level includes perceiving, making due, and identifying with our own sentiments and the sensations of others. The compass guides us through the occasionally wild oceans of our feelings.

**4. Embracing the Awkward

Similarly as the sun doesn't sparkle consistently, we will not necessarily in all cases feel good feelings. It's alright to sit with distress and investigate the shadows of our sentiments. Embracing the awkward is a valiant move toward self-revelation and development.

**5. The Language of Feelings

Sentiments impart important data about our necessities, wants, and limits. They are the language of our inward world. Focusing on this close to home language permits us to answer with shrewdness and realness.

**6. Profound Versatility

Life's process is sprinkled with difficulties that mix the close to home waters. Building profound strength resembles wearing a solid waterproof shell notwithstanding storms. It includes adjusting to misfortune, gaining from mishaps, and returning with newly discovered strength.

**7. Communicating Feelings

Finding sound source for our feelings is critical. Whether it's through craftsmanship, composing, conversing with a companion, or taking part in actual work, communicating feelings is the delivery valve that keeps inward tension from developing.

**8. Developing Positive Feelings

Similarly as a nursery expects care to blossom, our close to home prosperity benefits from the development of positive feelings. Participating in exercises that give pleasure, appreciation and chuckling adds to a thriving profound scene.

All in all, the lowdown on sentiments is a festival of the extravagance and intricacy that feelings bring to our lives. Embrace the variety of your profound scene, explore the ups and downs with interest and sympathy, and recall that feeling profoundly is a necessary piece of being human.

Part 2: Psychological well-being

Hello, before we jump into the quick and dirty of mental prosperity, how about we start by disentangling the secret of "Emotional well-being." You could have heard this term threw around, yet how might it truly affect us, the teens exploring the labyrinth of immaturity?

**The Brain Guide: Envision your psyche as a tremendous scene, loaded up with slopes and valleys, daylight and tempests. Psychological wellness resembles the weather conditions in this scene — everything revolves around how we feel within. At the point when our emotional well-being is great, it resembles a bright day, ready to go, lucidity, and energy. However, when tempest mists accumulate, it's OK to recognize the downpour, thunder, or even an intermittent lightning. That is a piece of being human.

**Profound Weather conditions Check: Our feelings resemble weather conditions. Joy, misery, fervor, stress, they go back and forth. Psychological well-being is tied in with understanding and dealing with these close to home weather conditions changes.

It's perceiving when a shady day may be transforming into a tempest and knowing how to explore through it.

**The Psyche Body Association: Here's a cool mystery, our brains and bodies resemble dearest companions who never go anyplace without one another. At the point when we discuss psychological well-being, we're additionally discussing what our contemplations and sentiments can mean for our actual prosperity. At any point saw how stress can cause your stomach to do somersaults or how a decent snicker can cause you to feel lighter? That is the psyche body association in real life.

**Difficult exercise: Very much like tumblers on a tightrope, keeping up with psychological wellness is a difficult exercise. It's figuring out the perfect balance where we can deal with life's difficulties, commend the triumphs, and know when to flimsy request help when things get a little. There's no need to focus on being great; it's tied in with being strong and figuring out how to move in the downpour when the tempests hit.

Thus, my companions, emotional wellness is the craft of grasping, embracing, and dealing with our inward scene. As we leave on this excursion together, we should recall that it's OK not to have every one of the responses, and posing inquiries is completely typical. The experience into psychological well-being is about self-disclosure, versatility, and the lovely, consistently adjusting embroidery of our perspectives. Prepared for the following part? How about we continue to investigate!

Part 3: The Four Essences of Psychological wellness

Okay, how about we jump further into the scene of our brains and investigate the four critical parts of psychological wellness. Consider these as various territories in the tremendous field of your psychological world.

**1. Close to home Prosperity:

This is the main issue at hand — how we experience and deal with our feelings. Close to home prosperity is tied in with figuring out the full range of sentiments, from happiness and energy to trouble and dissatisfaction. It resembles having a brilliant range of feelings and figuring out how to paint your own profound show-stopper.

**2. Social Prosperity: Similarly as trees need a woodland to flourish, we, as well, are social animals. Social prosperity is about our associations with others. Companions, family, and the more extensive local area assume pivotal parts in this viewpoint. It's structure an encouraging group of people, manufacturing significant connections, and establishing a positive social climate. All things considered, life's experiences are better when shared!

**3. Mental Prosperity:

Presently, we should wander into the domain of contemplations and mentalities. Mental prosperity includes the tales we tell ourselves, our confidence, and how we approach difficulties. It resembles having a tool kit loaded up with positive certifications, a development outlook, and a sprinkle of self-empathy. Exploring the exciting bends in the road of life turns out to be a lot of smoother when our psychological tool compartment is very much supplied.

**4. Conduct Prosperity:

Talk is cheap, correct? Social prosperity is about our ordinary propensities, how we deal with ourselves, and the decisions. It's the craft of tracking down balance — pursuing decisions that line up with our qualities and add to our general prosperity. From getting sufficient rest to taking part in exercises we love, our ways of behaving shape the scene of our emotional well-being.

As we investigate these four features, recollect that emotional wellness is certainly not a one-size-fits-all idea. Every one of us is a special magnum opus, and understanding these viewpoints assists us with painting our own energetic, developing image of prosperity. Thus, snatch your psychological compass, embrace the variety of your brain's landscape, and how about we proceed with this interesting excursion into the core of psychological wellness!

Part 4: Exploring the Tempest: Most ideal Ways to Control Your Psychological Boat

Okay, we've covered the lay of the land. Presently, we should head out into the immense ocean of procedures to keep our psychological ships consistent, particularly when the waters get unpleasant.

**1. Associate with Your Team:

Very much like a boat needs a group, we flourish when we're encircled by strong loved ones. Share your considerations and sentiments, and feel free to request help when you want it.

Social associations are like anchors — they keep us grounded during storms.

**2. Outline Your Course with Objectives:

Defining objectives provides our excursion guidance. Whether enormous or little, objectives give a feeling of motivation and accomplishment. Separate them into reasonable advances, and praise every achievement. It resembles having a guide for your psychological journey.

**3. Become the best at Taking care of oneself:

Dealing with your-self isn't an extravagance, it's a need. Whether it's a comfortable night with a decent book, a lively stroll in nature, or just stopping to inhale, taking care of oneself keeps your psychological boat in top condition.

**4. Weatherproof Your Psyche with Flexibility:

Tempests might come, yet versatility assists us with returning. Foster a versatile outlook by considering difficulties to be valuable chances to learn and develop. Like having a durable anchor keeps you consistent in rough oceans.

**5. Explore with Care:

At any point had a go at directing a boat without focusing on the compass? Care is your psychological compass. It's tied in with being available at the time, relinquishing stresses over the past or future. Embrace care rehearses like reflection or profound breathing to remain focused.

**6. Look for Proficient Direction

Exploring precarious waters could require an accomplished chief. Assuming the tempests appear to be overpowering, think about looking for help from psychological wellness experts. They have the information and apparatuses to direct you through difficult situations.

**7. Embrace the Force of Inspiration

Positive reasoning isn't tied in with disregarding difficulties; it's tied in with moving toward them with a confident outlook. Develop an uplifting perspective, encircle yourself with inspiration, and watch how it changes the air on board your psychological boat.

Keep in mind, each mariner faces tempests, and feeling a piece ocean wiped out sometimes is OK. The key is to outfit your-self with a strong mental boat and a tool stash of methodologies. In this way, raise your psychological anchor, get the breezes of prosperity, and how about we sail through the difficulties with fortitude and versatility.

Part 5: Anchors Away: Exploring Unpleasant Mental Waters

We've investigated the magnificence of mental prosperity, yet presently it is the ideal time to discuss how we can loan some assistance when our loved ones are confronting turbulent oceans. Supporting somebody with terrible emotional wellness resembles being a beacon, directing them securely to more quiet shores.

**1. Be an Attentive person

Now and then, all somebody needs is a listening ear. Be available, mindful, and open to hearing their considerations and sentiments. Keep away from judgment and deal compassion — it resembles tossing a life saver to somebody in tempestuous waters.

**2. Offer Your Empathy

Empathy is a strong power. Offer grace and understanding, perceiving that everybody's process is extraordinary. Demonstrations of empathy, huge or little, make waves of help that can have a tremendous effect.

**3. Energize Proficient Assistance: At the point when the waves get excessively high, reassuring looking for proficient support is fundamental. Specialists, instructors, and emotional wellness experts resemble talented guides who can give successful systems to a smoother venture.

**4. Remain Associated

Separation can be a tempest in itself. Remain associated with your companions or relatives going through a difficult stretch. Indeed, even a basic message or a common action can be a life saver, reminding them they're in good company in the tremendous ocean.

**5. Teach Yourself

Information is a strong partner. Find opportunity to find out about psychological well-being conditions and what they could mean for somebody. Understanding the difficulties they face resembles having a guide to explore the intricacies of their feelings.

**6. Show restraint, Be Available

Recuperating takes time. Show restraint toward your companion or relative and be available all through their excursion. Your resolute help resembles a tough anchor, keeping them grounded in snapshots of vulnerability.

**7. Break the Shame

How about we be pioneers in breaking down the walls of disgrace encompassing psychological wellness. Empower open discussions, share stories, and cultivate a climate where looking for help is viewed as an indication of solidarity.

**8. Encourage a Positive Climate

Make a good air where people around you have a solid sense of reassurance to communicate their sentiments. Little tokens of inspiration, similar to uplifting statements or thoughtful gestures, add to a better aggregate mental space.

Keep in mind, as an individual mariner in the ocean of life, your help can have a significant effect. By broadening some assistance, you become an encouraging sign, directing others toward the light on their emotional wellness venture. Thus, we should cruise together, cultivating a local area where sympathy and understanding are the breeze in our sails. Ahead, heroes of mental prosperity!

Part 6: Enlightening the Skyline: The Significance of Emotional wellness Mindfulness

In our investigation of mental prosperity, focusing a light on the benefit of emotional wellness awareness is pivotal. Envision mindfulness as the signal that punctures through the obscurity, scattering legends and encouraging a local area that embraces the different scenes of the brain.

**1. Ending the Quietness

Psychological wellness mindfulness is the way to ending the quiet that frequently covers emotional well-being issues. By straightforwardly examining our considerations and sentiments, we destroy the hindrances that propagate shame and make a space for certifiable discussions.

**2. Enabling People

Information is power, and with regards to psychological wellness, mindfulness engages people to assume responsibility for their prosperity. It furnishes us with the apparatuses to perceive when our psychological oceans are becoming wild and energizes proactive strides toward keeping up with great emotional well-being.

**3. Lessening Shame and Misguided judgments

Disgrace resembles a mist that clouds understanding. Emotional wellness mindfulness lifts this haze, dispersing confusions and encouraging a climate where people have a real sense of security to look for help unafraid of judgment. It's an aggregate work to make a world liberated from the shackles of disgrace.

**4. Making Strong People group

Mindfulness fabricates extensions of sympathy and empathy, encouraging strong networks where people feel comprehended and acknowledged. At the point when we know about the battles looked by others, we can expand some assistance and make an organization of fortitude.

**5. Encouraging Early Intercession

Similarly as we address actual wellbeing concerns expeditiously, psychological wellness mindfulness empowers early intercession. Perceiving the indications of mental trouble considers opportune help, keeping difficulties from growing into additional complicated issues.

**6. Teaching and Sympathizing: is established in training and compassion. By understanding the different idea of psychological well-being, we develop a feeling of sympathy that rises above judgment. This schooling enables us to remain as supporters, advancing mental prosperity as a key part of in general wellbeing.

**7. Empowering Taking care of oneself

Emotional wellness mindfulness features the significance of taking care of oneself practices. At the point when people know about the effect of way of life decisions on their psychological prosperity, they can take on procedures that advance versatility, stress decrease, and in general mental thriving.

**8. Backing for Strategy Change

An aggregate voice filled by mindfulness can drive strategy change. By pushing for emotional wellness mindfulness at a cultural level, we add to strategies that focus on emotional wellness in schools, working environments, and networks, establishing conditions that support prosperity.

All in all, psychological well-being mindfulness isn't simply a flame in the obscurity; a group of stars guides us toward a future where each individual's psychological prosperity is recognized, upheld, and celebrated. As we convey this light forward, we should enlighten the skyline, rousing a reality where psychological wellness isn't simply perceived however loved as a fundamental piece of the human experience.

Part 7: The Specialty of Flourishing: Characterizing Prosperity

Now that we've ventured through the scenes of psychological well-being, now is the right time to set our compass on the idea of prosperity. Envision prosperity as the energetic nursery inside the immense domain of our lives, thriving with the products of bliss, satisfaction, and reason.

**1. Encompassing Embroidery

Prosperity is something beyond the shortfall of disease; an encompassing embroidery winds around together different parts of our lives. Actual wellbeing, mental prosperity, social associations, and a feeling of direction all add to the rich texture of prosperity.

**2. Actual Imperativeness

The first brushstroke in our prosperity show-stopper is actual wellbeing. It includes dealing with our bodies through customary activity, adjusted nourishment, adequate rest, and careful propensities. At the point when our bodies flourish, so does our general prosperity.

**3. Profound Concordance

Close to home prosperity paints the material with energetic tints of euphoria, versatility, and mindfulness. It's tied in with understanding, communicating, and dealing with our feelings in a way that improves our daily routines and the existences of everyone around us.

**4. Social Associations

Prosperity blooms in the prolific soil of social associations. Significant connections, positive co-operations, and a feeling of having a place add to the feeling of local area that sustains our prosperity. Like blossoms in a nursery, our associations sprout and prosper.

**5. Mental Flexibility

A strong psyche is the foundation of prosperity. There's really no need to focus on keeping away from difficulties yet fostering the strength to explore them. Prosperity embraces a positive outlook, versatile survival methods, and a readiness to learn and develop through life's exciting bends in the road.

**6. Reason and Importance

At any point seen a nursery without reason? Neither does prosperity. Having a feeling of direction, an explanation that fills our interests and drives our activities, adds profundity and wealth to our lives. The anchor keeps us grounded in the tempests.

**7. Monetary Strength

While not the whole nursery, monetary security is a crucial rose in the bundle of prosperity. It includes overseeing assets carefully, anticipating the future, and developing a sound connection with cash to decrease pressure and advance security.

**8. Ecological Prosperity

The strength of our environmental elements impacts our prosperity. A spotless, safe, and practical climate upholds our physical and psychological well-being. Being aware of our effect in the world is like watching out for the roots that sustain our prosperity.

Basically, prosperity is a no nonsense magnum opus that we create all through our lives. It's tied in with sustaining every part of our reality and tracking down amicability in the ensemble of physical, close to home, social, and mental components. Thus, we should keep an eye on our nurseries with care, develop the seeds of prosperity, and watch as they sprout into a day to day existence loaded up with reason, euphoria, and satisfaction. Forward, landscapers of prosperity!

Part 8: The Craft of Self-Sustaining: Divulging the Genuine Quintessence of Taking care of oneself

In the mosaic of prosperity, taking care of oneself is the delicate brushstroke that adds energy and equilibrium. We should set out on an excursion to uncover the genuine importance of taking care of oneself, dispersing fantasies and embracing the real practices that sustain our psyches, bodies, and spirits.

**1. Embracing the Entire Self

Taking care of oneself isn't an extravagance; it's an essential thoughtful gesture to yourself. It includes perceiving and regarding your physical, profound, and mental necessities. Picture it as a safe-haven where you can re-energize, refuel, and reconnect with your deepest self.

**2. Custom fitted to You

One size doesn't fit all in that frame of mind of taking care of oneself. What carries serenity to one individual might be different for another. Taking care of oneself is profoundly private, and finding what impacts you resembles finding the ideal tune for your prosperity.

**3. Day to day Demonstrations of Adoration

In spite of prevalent thinking, taking care of oneself isn't generally excellent signals. It's generally expected tracked down in the little, day to day demonstrations of adoration towards yourself. Whether it's relishing some tea, going for a short stroll, or partaking in a decent book, these minutes add to your general prosperity.

**4. Limits as Strongholds

Defining limits is a foundation of taking care of oneself. There's no need to focus on saying "no" to other people; it's tied in with saying "OK" to yourself. Laying out limits on your significant investment guarantees that you can immerse your own cup prior to offering it to other people.

**5. Careful Presence

Taking care of oneself is moored in care. Being completely present at the time, without judgment, is a strong type of self-supporting. It permits you to see the value in the wealth of your encounters and develop a profound association with yourself.

**6. Rest and Reclamation

Genuine taking care of oneself perceives the significance of rest and reclamation. In a world that commends stress, getting some margin to rest resembles permitting your body and mind to recuperate. It's an interest in your drawn out prosperity.

**7. Saying "OK" to Self-Revelation

Taking part in exercises that give you pleasure and satisfaction is a type of self-revelation. Whether it's seeking after a side interest, discovering some new information, or basically getting some margin for reflection, taking care of oneself is the compass that guides you on an excursion to be aware and love yourself better.

**8. Looking for Help When Required

Taking care of oneself isn't generally an independent mission. Perceiving when you want backing and connecting for help is a crucial viewpoint. Whether from companions, family, or experts, tolerating support is a brave demonstration of taking care of oneself. Fundamentally, taking care of oneself is a main avenue for affection spoken straightforwardly to your spirit. It's tied in with cultivating a humane relationship with yourself, recognizing that you deserve a similar consideration and consideration you promptly proposition to other people. Thus, how about we unwind the layers of taking care of oneself, embracing the genuineness of these practices as we explore the delightful mosaic of prosperity.

Part 9: The Taking care of oneself Orchestra: Practices for Each Aspect of Your Life

Now that we comprehend the quintessence of taking care of oneself, we should investigate an orchestra of practices that resound with every part of our lives. Picture this as a playlist, organized to carry congruity to your whole self.

**1. Actual Desert spring

- **Development Sorcery: Whether it's a dance meeting, yoga, or a tranquil walk, let your body depression and stretch. Actual development resembles an adoration tune to your muscles and joints.

- **Sustenance Customs: Treat your body to healthy feasts that fuel and fulfill. Establish a sustaining climate for your feasts, relishing each chomp like a culinary orchestra.

- **Reviving Rest: Focus on quality rest, lay out a sleep time schedule that signs to your body that now is the ideal time to loosen up and embrace the calming tune of rest.

**2. Profound Agreement

- **Journaling Excursion: Record your considerations and sentiments. It resembles making the verses out of your close to home soundtrack, permitting you to reflect and deliver.

- **Imaginative Articulation: Participate in exercises that permit your feelings to stream. Whether it's painting, music, or composing verse, let your inventiveness dance unreservedly.

- **Careful Relaxing: Take minutes over the course of the day to deliberately relax. This training is a relieving cadence for your close to home prosperity.

**3. Social Tranquility

- **Quality Time: Put resources into significant associations. Plan time with loved ones, developing the amicable bonds that inspire your soul.

- **Computerized Detox: Make spaces of calm in your social circle. Turn off from the advanced commotion and let the real associations around you become the overwhelming focus.

- **Thoughtful gestures: Spread inspiration. Little thoughtful gestures make a gradually expanding influence, enhancing both your life and the existences of everyone around you.

**4. Mental Thriving

- **Learning Ensemble: Draw in your brain with interest. Whether it's perusing, mastering another expertise, or settling puzzles, keep your psychological pinion wheels turning.

- **Careful Breaks: Enjoy short reprieves during the day to reset. It very well may be a couple of moments of profound breathing or a snapshot of care to recalibrate your psychological compass.

- **Objective Setting Melody: Put forth sensible objectives that line up with your qualities. Breaking them into feasible advances makes a delightful cadence of progress.

**5. Deliberate Investigation

- **Energy Pursuits: Devote time to exercises that give you pleasure. Seeking after your interests resembles making the song out of direction in your life.

- **Objective Driven Experience: Put forth and seek after objectives that line up with your qualities and goals. It resembles diagramming a course toward the satisfaction of your life's motivation.

- **Intelligent Retreat: Take minutes for reflection. A customary retreat into your viewpoints and yearnings makes an agreeable association with your life's motivation.

Keep in mind, the taking care of oneself ensemble is an always developing organization. Tweak this playlist to suit your one of a kind mood and let the practices in every part of your life make a show-stopper of prosperity.

Part 10: The Mainstays of Taking care of oneself: Building Areas of strength for a for Prosperity

As we dive further into the craft of taking care of oneself, we should investigate the seven support points that structure the tough groundwork of a versatile and thriving life. These support points are the underlying components that, when coordinated into your everyday daily schedule, make a strong structure for sustaining your whole self.

**1. Actual Health Point of support

Building Serious areas of strength for a Foundation

Actual taking care of oneself is the foundation of prosperity. It includes sustaining your body through solid propensities, development, and rest. The actual health point of support incorporates:

- **Sustenance: Fuel your body with healthy, sustaining food varieties that give the energy and supplements it needs.

- **Work out: Integrate customary active work into your daily practice, whether it's an energetic walk, an exercise meeting, or a dance break.

- **Serene Rest: Focus on quality rest to permit your body and mind to re-energize and revive.

**2. Close to home Strength Support point

Reinforcing the Core of Well-Being

Close to home taking care of oneself spotlights on getting it, communicating, and dealing with your feelings in a solid manner. The profound flexibility point of support incorporates:

- **Care Practices: Develop consciousness of your viewpoints and sentiments through care reflection or profound breathing activities.

- **Imaginative Articulation: Participate in exercises that permit you to communicate and deal with your feelings, for example, journaling, workmanship, or music.

- **Positive Insistences: Encourage a positive mentality by consolidating certifications that elevate and motivate.

**3. Social Association Point of support

Building Scaffolds for a Strong Network

Social taking care of oneself accentuates the significance of significant associations and strong connections. The social association point of support includes:

- **Quality Time: Invest energy with loved ones, sustaining connections that give pleasure and backing.

- **Advanced Detox: Enjoy reprieves from computerized interruptions to interface really with people around you.

- **Thoughtful gestures: Spread energy by taking part in thoughtful gestures, both of all shapes and sizes.

**4. Mental Clearness Point of support

Honing the Focal point of Your Mind

Mental taking care of oneself is tied in with keeping up with mental wellbeing and encouraging reliable. The psychological clearness point of support incorporates:

- **Learning and Development: Take part in exercises that animate your psyche and energize continuous learning.

- **Careful Breaks: Enjoy short reprieves to reset and forestall mental exhaustion.

- **Objective Setting: Put forth reasonable objectives that line up with your qualities, giving a feeling of motivation and heading.

**5. Profound Sustenance Point of support

Taking care of the Spirit's Yearning for Meaning

Otherworldly taking care of oneself includes interfacing with your internal identity, values, and a feeling of direction. The otherworldly sustenance support point includes:

- **Careful Reflection: Take minutes for thoughtfulness and examination, encouraging a more profound comprehension of your qualities and convictions

- **Nature Connection: Spend time in nature to cultivate a sense of awe and connection to something greater.

- **Intentional Living: Adjust your activities to your qualities, embracing a deliberate and significant presence.

**6. Time Usage Point of support

Making Equilibrium in the Orchestra of Life

Compelling using time effectively is a vital part of taking care of oneself, guaranteeing that you designate time for the main thing. The time usage point of support incorporates:

- **Prioritization: Recognize your needs and designate time in like manner, zeroing in on what gives you pleasure and satisfaction.

- **Limits: Put down solid stopping points to safeguard your significant investment, forestalling burnout.

- **Careful Booking: Plan your days carefully, considering a harmony between work, relaxation, and taking care of oneself.

**7. Rest and Unwinding Support point

Re-energizing the Batteries of Well-Being

Rest and unwinding are indispensable parts of taking care of oneself, giving the space to revival. The rest and unwinding support point includes:

- **Quality Free time: Timetable purposeful times of rest, permitting your psyche and body to loosen up.

- **Recreation Exercises: Participate in exercises only for satisfaction, whether it's perusing, watching a film, or washing up.

- **Profound Unwinding Strategies: Integrate profound unwinding rehearses, like moderate muscle unwinding or directed symbolism, to deliver pressure and advance serenity.

As you incorporate these seven support points into your everyday daily schedule, imagine them as the durable segments supporting the design of your prosperity. Every point of support adds to the strength and flexibility of the construction, making an amicable space where you can flourish.

Part 11: The Prosperity Profits: Finding the Advantages of Taking care of oneself

As we proceed with our excursion through the domains of prosperity, how about we disentangle the heap compensates that unfurl when we embrace the specialty of taking care of oneself. Consider these advantages the blooms that sprout in the nursery of your life, each adding to the lively embroidered artwork of your general prosperity.

1. Improved Actual Wellbeing

- **Helped Insusceptibility: Normal taking care of oneself practices, like satisfactory rest, adjusted nourishment, and exercise, add to a hearty resistant framework, sustaining your body's protections.

- **Expanded Energy Levels: Supporting your actual prosperity through taking care of oneself outcomes in higher energy levels, permitting you to move toward every day with essentialness and excitement.

- **Further developed Rest Quality: Laying out sleep time schedules and rehearsing unwinding methods add to all the more likely rest, advancing generally actual revival.

**2. Raised Profound Prosperity

- **Stress Decrease Ensemble: Taking part in taking care of oneself exercises, for example, care and unwinding rehearses, oversees feelings of anxiety and cultivates close to home versatility.

- **Improved Capacity to appreciate people on a profound level: Ordinary reflection and close to home articulation through taking care of oneself add to an increased comprehension and the executives of your own feelings.

- **Cheerful State of mind Symphony: Seeking after exercises that give you pleasure and unwinding adds to a positive state of mind, establishing an agreeable profound climate.

**3. Reinforced Social Associations

- **Quality Connections: When you focus on taking care of oneself, you carry the best version of yourself to your connections, encouraging further associations with others.

- **Sympathy Enhancement: Taking care of oneself improves your profound prosperity, permitting you to be more present and sympathetic in your communications with loved ones.

-**Limits as Extensions: Defining and keeping up with limits through taking care of oneself practices makes better, more adjusted connections.

**4. Honed Mental Concentration

- **Expanded Efficiency: A very much refreshed brain and body, upheld by taking care of oneself practices, add to improved concentration and efficiency in everyday errands.

- **Upgraded Mental Capability: Normal mental breaks and care rehearses help in streamlining mental capability, supporting more clear reasoning and direction.

- **Embracing Innovativeness: Taking care of oneself gives the psychological space and unwinding required for imaginative reasoning and critical thinking.

**5. Intentional Living

- **Lucidity of Direction: Participating in taking care of oneself practices considers reflection, adding to a more clear comprehension of your qualities and life objectives. **Resilience in Pursuit: Taking care of oneself supports versatility, giving the strength and inspiration expected to defeat difficulties and seek after your life's motivation.

- **Expanded Fulfillment: Living in arrangement with your motivation and values, worked with by taking care of oneself, prompts more noteworthy life fulfillment and satisfaction.

Fundamentally, the advantages of taking care of oneself reach out a long ways past fleeting unwinding; they are the profits that compound after some time, enhancing each feature of your life. As you watch out for the nursery of your prosperity, may you receive the abundant benefits of self-sustaining.

Conclusion: An Orchestra of Prosperity

As we arrive at the last notes of our investigation into the domains of emotional wellness, prosperity, and taking care of oneself, how about we respite to see the value in the tune we've formed together. This excursion has been an orchestra, fitting the different components that shape our lives into an embroidery of versatility, reason, and satisfaction. We've explored the scenes of psychological well-being, perceiving its multifaceted subtleties and the significance of cultivating our very own merciful comprehension minds. The sections unfurled like developments in a fabulous ensemble, each adding to the rich organization of prosperity.

From the investigation of close to home climate to the encouraging of strong networks, we've found the interconnectedness of our psychological, profound, social, and actual prosperity. We've commended the exceptional tune of taking care of oneself, understanding that it's anything but an extravagance however a major thoughtful gesture to ourselves. The practices we've uncovered are the notes that make a relieving concordance, resounding in each part of our lives.

In our mission to characterize prosperity, we've embraced the all en-compassing nature of a daily routine very much experienced — supporting our bodies, grasping our feelings, cultivating significant associations, and chasing after a deliberate presence. The sections have unfurled like petals in a blossoming garden, each adding to the dynamic bundle of a thriving life.

The advantages of taking care of oneself, similar to the sweet holds back of a wonderfully played instrument, are the gifts we present to ourselves. Upgraded actual wellbeing, raised profound prosperity, reinforced social associations, honed mental concentration, and deliberate living are the rich profits of our self-sustaining tries.

As we close this ensemble, let us convey the examples learned and rehearses embraced into the crescendo of our day to day routines. May we keep on sustaining our psychological scenes, watch out for the nurseries of our prosperity, and play the music of taking care of oneself with bliss and aim.

Keep in mind, the guide of your prosperity is, in all honesty, yourself. As you explore the oceans of life, may you track down comfort in the tunes of self-empathy, strength in the harmonies of association, and reason in the coordination of your remarkable life melody.

Forward, May your process be loaded up with the sweet tunes of delight, the full harmonies of satisfaction, and the persevering through rhythms of a daily routine very much experienced.